W9-AQV-612

Date: 3/19/13

Marine Mammals

Bottlenose Dolphins

by Jody Sullivan Rake

Consulting editor: Gail Saunders-Smith, PhD

CAPSTONE PRESS
a capstone imprint

Pebble Plus is published by Capstone Publishers,
1710 Roe Crest Drive, North Mankato, MN 56003
www.capstonepub.com

Library of Congress Cataloging-in-Publication Data
Rake, Jody Sullivan.
Bottlenose Dolphins / by Jody Sullivan Rake.
p. cm.—(Pebble plus. Marine mammals)
Includes bibliographical references and index.
Summary: "Simple text and full-color photographs provide a brief introduction to
bottlenose dolphins"—Provided by publisher.
ISBN 978-1-4296-8716-4 (hardcover)
ISBN 978-1-62065-310-4 (eBook PDF)
1. Bottlenose dolphin—Juvenile literature. I. Title.

QL737.C432P463 2013
599.53'3—dc23   2012002626

Editorial Credits
Jeni Wittrock, editor; Ted Williams, designer; Svetlana Zhurkin, media researcher; Kathy McColley,production specialist

Photo Credits
Alamy: imagebroker, 7, Picture Press, 9; Dreamstime: Brandon Bourdages, 13; Getty Images: Jeff Rotman, 19;
iStockphoto: Brett Charlton, 15, Craig Dingle, 11; Newscom: Danita Delimont Photography/Franklin Viola, 5;
Shutterstock: abracadabra (dolphin), 8, Alexey Sokolov, cover, Beth Schroeder, 3, Dray van Beeck, 17, mcherevan
(splash), cover, 1, Mikhail Dudarev (water texture), cover, 1, Sergey Shumakov, 21

Note to Parents and Teachers

The Marine Mammals series supports national science standards related to life science.
This book describes and illustrates bottlenose dolphins. The images support early readers in
understanding the text. The repetition of words and phrases helps early readers learn new
words. This book also introduces early readers to subject-specific vocabulary words, which are
defined in the Glossary section. Early readers may need assistance to read some words and to
use the Table of Contents, Glossary, Read More, Internet Sites, and Index sections of the book.

Printed in the United States of America in North Mankato, Minnesota.
042012   006682CGF12

Table of Contents

Jumping the Waves

A bottlenose dolphin springs out of the waves. This marine mammal leaps into the air as high as 16 feet (4.9 meters).

Bottlenose dolphins live in warm ocean water. Bottlenoses swim near Florida, Texas, and southern California.

Bottlenose Dolphin Range

where bottlenose dolphins swim

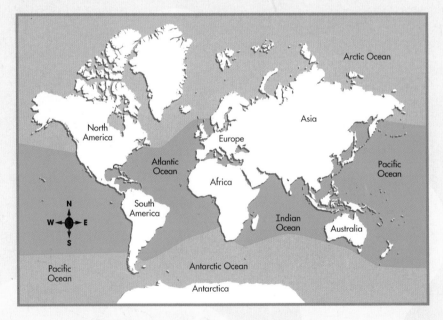

7

A Bottlenose Dolphin's Body

A bottlenose dolphin is built for speed. Its body is shaped like a rocket. Its slippery gray skin cuts through the water.

Bottlenose dolphin:
12 feet (3.7 meters) long

5 feet (1.5 m) long

When dolphins swim,
their strong tails pump up
and down. Their flippers steer.
Dolphins' tall dorsal fins
help them balance.

Bottlenose dolphins have smooth, bottle-shaped snouts. Dolphins have 100 small, sharp teeth to help catch slippery fish.

A blowhole on its head

helps a dolphin breathe

at the water's surface.

A strong flap covers

the blowhole under water.

Life at Sea

Bottlenose dolphins use
echolocation to find prey.
Bottlenoses make high noises.
If sounds bounce back,
there might be food ahead.

Dolphin Life Cycle

Baby bottlenoses are
about 4 feet (1.2 m) long.
Young bottlenose dolphins
stay with their mothers
for about six years.

Mothers and their young
live in groups of two
to 15 bottlenoses. Adult males
have their own groups.
Bottlenoses live 20 to 25 years.

Glossary

blowhole—a hole on the top of a dolphin's head; dolphins breathe air through blowhole

dorsal fin—the fin that sticks up from the middle of a dolphin's back

echolocation—the process of using sounds and echoes to locate objects; dolphins use echolocation to find food

flipper—one of the broad, flat limbs of a sea creature

mammal—a warm-blooded animal that breathes air; mammals have hair or fur; female mammals feed milk to their young

marine—living in salt water

prey—an animal hunted by another animal for food

snout—the long front part of an animal's head that includes the nose, mouth, and jaws

Read More

Clark, Willow. *Dolphins: Life in the Pod.* Animal Families.
New York: PowerKids Press, 2011.

De Medeiros, James. *Dolphins.* Amazing Animals.
New York: Weigl Publishers, 2009.

Shaskan, Trisha Speed. *What's the Difference between a Dolphin and a Porpoise?* What's the Difference?
Mankato, Minn.: Picture Window Books, 2011.

Internet Sites

FactHound offers a safe, fun way to find Internet sites related to this book. All of the sites on FactHound have been researched by our staff.

Here's all you do:

Visit *www.facthound.com*

Type in this code: 9781429687164

23

Index

Word Count: 181
Grade: 1
Early-Intervention Level: 16